MY T-REX GETS A BATH

CHLOE SANDERS

MY T- REX GETS A BATH

BY CHLOE SANDERS

THANK YOU!

FOR PURCHASING THIS BOOK,

I'D LIKE TO GIVE YOU A FREE GIFT

A GREAT FUN AND ADVENTURE BOOK FOR YOUR CHILD

HERE YOU CAN GET YOUR FREE GIFT!

HTTPS://TESTKUSTOV.LEADPAGES.CO/FREEBOOK-KIDS/

TOM AND HIS DINOSAUR LOVED TO PLAY

UNTIL IT CAME TO THE END OF THE DAY

WHEN MUM SAID, "IT'S TIME TO GET READY FOR BED."

BUT REX HAD FAR DIFFERENT PLANS INSTEAD.

MUM SAID, "IT'S TIME TO PUT BACK YOUR TOYS."

SHE FILLED THE BATH FOR THE TWO LITTLE BOYS.

BUT REX PULLED THE PLUG AND EMPTIED THE TUB.

HE GIGGLED AND SAID, "WE DON'T WANT TO SCRUB!"

"FORGET THE BATH. SEND THE WATER AWAY.

I KNOW A BETTER GAME WE CAN PLAY."

HE PRETENDED THE SOAP WAS SOME TREASURE HE'D FOUND

BUT IT SLIPPED FROM HIS HANDS AND DROPPED ON THE GROUND.

"BRUSHING YOUR TEETH IS BORING." REX SAID.

"HERE'S A GAME WE CAN PLAY INSTEAD."

REX OPENED THE TOOTHPASTE AND SQUIRTED SOME OUT.

"LOOK. IT'S A HOSE WITH A GREAT BIG SPOUT."

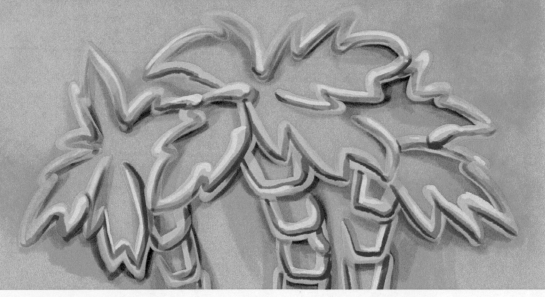

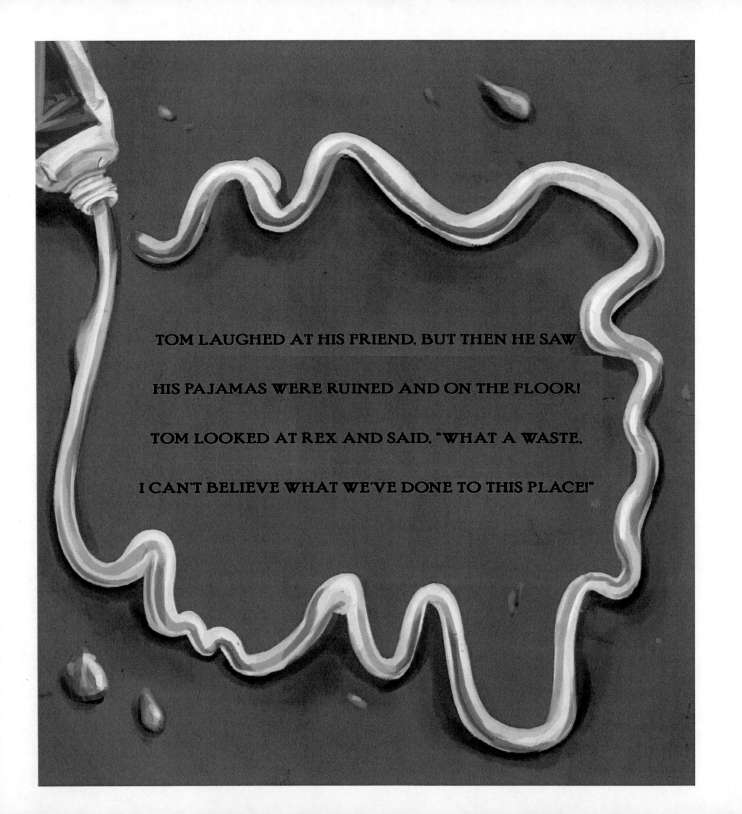

TOM LAUGHED AT HIS FRIEND. BUT THEN HE SAW

HIS PAJAMAS WERE RUINED AND ON THE FLOOR!

TOM LOOKED AT REX AND SAID, "WHAT A WASTE.

I CAN'T BELIEVE WHAT WE'VE DONE TO THIS PLACE!"

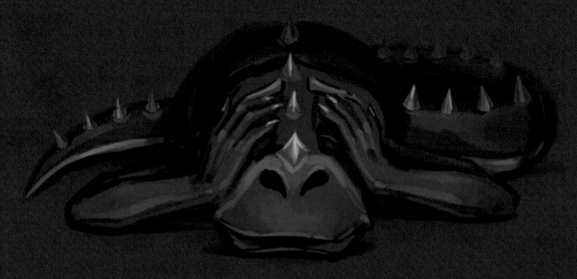

"I JUST WANTED TO PLAY," REX SAID.

THEN HE RAN TO HIDE UNDER TOM'S BED.

TOM WASN'T GOING TO TAKE THE BLAME.

IT WAS REX WHO HAD WANTED TO PLAY A GAME!

"IT'S TIME TO TEACH REX THAT HYGIENE IS FUN.

IT'S GOOD TO GET CLEAN WHEN THE DAY IS DONE."

HE PULLED REX OUT FROM UNDER THE BED.

"I HAVE A GREAT NEW GAME." HE SAID.

TOM GAVE A GRIN AS HE CLIMBED IN THE BATH.

SQUIRTING WATER AT REX, WHO STARTED TO LAUGH.

HE JUMPED IN WITH TOM TO SPLASH AND HAVE FUN.

THEY GOT WASHED WHILE PLAYING AND SOON THEY WERE DONE.

"COME ON THEN. REX - WHO CAN BRUSH THEIR TEETH QUICKER?"

REX JOINED IN WITH A SMILE AND A SNICKER

THEY GOT THEIR TEETH SHINING WHILE HAVING A RACE

AND SOON THEY BOTH HAD BRIGHT SMILES ON THEIR FACE.

MUM TUCKED THEM INTO TOM'S COSY BED,

SHE READ THEM A STORY AND KISSED THEIR HEADS.

REX WAS GLAD THEY GOT CLEAN AS THEY SHOULD,

AND THANKED TOM FOR TEACHING HIM THAT HYGIENE IS GOOD.

40442421R00015

Made in the USA
San Bernardino, CA
19 October 2016